Creative Healing

How God Helped Me Heal My Trauma
with the Gift of Creativity

TINA MELTON

Fulton Books
Meadville, PA

Published by Fulton Books 2022

ISBN 978-1-63985-286-4 (paperback)
ISBN 978-1-63985-287-1 (digital)

Printed in the United States of America

First, I want to thank God for saving me and giving me so many chances at life.

I dedicate this book to my sweet grandmother, Marjorie Smith, who nurtured my love for writing and art and my daughter, Angelia Pena, who is my angel God gave me.

I also want to give thanks to my mom, Janet Aleman, and my aunt, Judy Ireland. This dream would not have been possible without them.

I also thank my fiancé, Billy Clough, for his love and support and my sisters—Tanya Kelley, Misty Melton, Salena Aleman, and Sierra Aleman—for their love and support as well. I also thank all my other family; my dad, Nicky Melton; my granny Luan Melton; and all other family and friends.

CONTENTS

INTRODUCTION

What Is Creative Healing?

As I reflect on my life, I wonder how I ever made it through. Then I look at all my artworks and notebooks. I know it was the gift of creativity God gave me to help me heal from trauma. It has been imperative to my recovery. I want to share a journey with you how to use creativity as a healing method to whatever you are going through or have gone through in the past. I wrote this book to inspire healing by being creative. It has helped me since I was diagnosed with mental illness twenty-six years ago. It has been a process through the years. I started by writing in a journal in the year 2000. I have written about fifty notebooks since then. I started art therapy the first time I went to a state hospital for mental illness. I don't know what I would do without my creative outlets. They are really helpful when you are ill, whether it is mental, physical, emotional, or something else. I want to take you on an adventure to find your creative healing.

I read an article by Drew Barrymore one time, and it really inspired me. I hope it will inspire you as well. "You can go through life victimized and bitter, but that is such a waste. The best thing you can do is turn pain into strength, try to be a positive force, and make the most of this life you have been given. Cherish every day, every breath, and try to breathe that back into the world in making a family or being artistic. Just make the most of your life. The only person who will stop you is you." Isn't this so true? It really resonated with me. I especially love how it says turn pain into strength, try

7

to be a positive force, and make the most of this life you have been given. We all have pain at some point in our lives. It is unfortunately inevitable as human beings, but we have the ability to turn pain into strength by being artistic, raising a family, or whatever it is we desire. If we really open our eyes and our hearts with faith, we can move mountains. That is exhilarating to me.

This book is about using creativity to overcome whatever you may be struggling through. Maybe you would just like some tips to be more creative. There can be many perspectives how to view it.

Art is seeing. You have the option to open your eyes to new perspectives. To be an artist is to live and feel, then to express, to see things in everyday life you don't usually see. God created an amazing, beautiful world. Life is what you make of it, so look around with eyes always open. You have to use your senses: touch, taste, smell, see, hear, and the sixth one, intuition. We have to use our imagination and imagine the possibilities. Inspiration can spark a fire anywhere and in many forms. Imagination is the spice of life. Ask what if. Have the curious mind of a child. Believe in yourself. Dare to be different. Let your spirit fly. Get on your train of thought and let it take you places. Imagination is the key to open new doors. Think of your mind as a castle or the house of your dreams. There are many doors to open if you just free your mind. Allow it to wander through unknown territories.

Creative Healing is a book about believing, being *you*nique, seeing many sides of yourself, having variety in your life, using your imagination, and making your dreams come true. There is a child in all of us who wants to be creative and play. Children use their imaginations frequently. As we get older, sometimes we lose that child in us that helps us to play make believe and pretend. We get bogged down by finances, relationships, work, family, and whatever curveball life throws at us. We aren't doomed to a dull and boring life. We just have to rekindle the relationship with the child we once were or would have liked to have been.

There are some exercises in here that you don't have to do, but I would suggest you give them a try. Some might seem silly or ridiculous, but remember, the creative side of you is a child. Let the child play!

CHAPTER 1

Let in the Magic

What were you like as a child? Do you remember? What did you like to play with? Who was your best friend? Do you remember pretending? What did you want to be? Did you become it?

This section is all about letting in your inner child out to play. As adults, sometimes we lose the "magic" of discovering new things. We can become cynical and bitter. We are moody and stressed out. Maybe the job is stressful for you, bills pile up, or your relationships aren't going the way you hoped. Maybe you have an illness that keeps you depressed. All these things can put a damper on living, but I have learned we don't have to let it control us. The mind can be a magical place to go to if we let it in. It can be a fun-filled amusement park. Think about going to the carnival or an amusement park. All right, don't think about the money you will have to spend. Think about the fun things there. Imagine you are a kid again and remember the feeling you got when you first went to one. Do you remember your first ride or roller coaster? Did you like it? Was it scary? Would you do it again? Do you remember the excitement you felt? Do you remember eating cotton candy and funnel cakes without worrying about your weight? Do you remember the games? Imagine that for a minute. How has going changed for you now?

Do you still enjoy going or do you worry about the money you are going to have to spend? Do you remember the thrill of going to a new place or somewhere you really enjoyed? Let the kid in you enjoy new ventures. It does not have to be a place for children. It could be a new restaurant but enjoy it like your younger self would.

I used to love to sing and dance. I was told I had a very good voice. I would go all over the house singing and dancing happily. As I got older and was told I didn't sing very well, I became self-conscious about it, so I stopped for a while. But I realized I still love to do it, so I did it. I don't let negative comments or ridicules bother me anymore because it is something I love to do. Don't let negativity or ridicule stop you from doing the things you enjoy. If you love to sing, sing. If you love to dance, dance. If you love to write off the wall stories, write them anyway. I would love to read them. My point is, do what is in your heart. Don't let people's opinions or your self-conscience destroy what you love to do. This is a quote I created about shining. Find your star, pull it out of your pocket, let it sparkle, shine, and light up a room.

I love *Alice in Wonderland* by Lewis Carrol. Anybody who really knows me knows this. I love his style of writing and his imagination. He was so imaginative and such a creative genius. My life has felt like a wonderland, at times so animated yet so confusing. Mental illness can feel this way. It has almost felt like a movie. I've had dreams I was in Wonderland. Monsters were after me, then I turned into a fairy and flew away. Sometimes our lives make no sense at all. Somewhere there is an answer to our problems. I learned it wasn't from any kind of chemical. I believe it is faith in our heavenly Father and in our imagination of what can be. I think I would go absolutely bonkers without my imagination of the possibilities in life.

There are many ways to figure out what is in your imagination. You can brainstorm, role-play, keep a creativity journal, read inspiring stories, have a variety of hobbies, and lots more. These are just a few things. What do you like to think about when you let your mind wonder? What inspires you? Do you like art, music, science, history, literature, or something else? I love to make art, writing, and music. These are my three favorite hobbies. What are yours? You can brainstorm this by listing all the things you love, then you can narrow down your top three.

Role-playing is another way to ponder what you enjoy. Who is your favorite role model? It can be anyone. It can be someone you are very close to or a celebrity you admire, dead or alive. What if you could talk to them for a day? What would you ask them? How would your life be different? What would you do differently than you are doing now? What if you were an actor or an actress? What role in a movie would you like to play? What kind of movie would it be? What if you were a songwriter? What songs would you write? What would they be about? What if you were a scientist? What would you like to discover? This is the good stuff of how we figure out what we imagine ourselves to be. What if you were a deep-sea explorer?

I'm sure you would have numerous things to talk about. What if you were a photographer for National Geographic? I think that would be fascinating. What if you were able to get into a shark cage with an eighteen-foot great white shark? Would you do it? It would be terrifying, but if I knew I would not be devoured by the shark, I would. I think it would be amazing to be so close to such a powerful beast of the waters. These are things I like to think about. What do you like to think about when you let your mind wander? Are you too worried about the stress and struggle of life to ponder other things? Of course you have to find solutions to your problems, but it is good to take a break and let your mind wander about the universe. It is an awesome universe we live in! There are so many amazing discoveries. This is why I am so passionate about art and writing. There is always something new to discover or create. It can be whatever you want it to be. I love killer whales, so it inspired me to paint a picture of one in teal-colored water. I think it is really beautiful, and it humbles me how I am just a speck of sand in this awesome world. I also enjoy abstract images to paint. It reminds me that not everything is always what it seems.

Art became therapy for me to cope with mental illness. I have painted many things to express myself. It is like a breath of fresh air when I express what I am thinking or feeling in something that is my own unique creation. I have a collection of writing prompts to write. I use them when I am having writer's block or to get ideas about what to write. They are all over the internet as apps or books to buy. You can google creative writing prompts, and a variety of them will appear. Sometimes, inspiration comes in unusual circumstances. On New Year's Day, a couple of years ago, I felt a twitch in my ear, then I had an idea for a story that a tiny airplane with tiny trolls flew into my ear and entered my brain. Inside of my brain was a castle. It sounds silly, but inspiration can spark a flame anywhere. I also created a writing prompt for a love letter from jelly to peanut butter. It was a little vulgar but comical nonetheless. I was very happy with its originality. I think writing and art is extremely liberating. I never know where my pen will take me, but I love not knowing. It's like the pen has a mind of its own. It takes off like a rocket to the moon, and I am on a new adventure. I may be floating through the air in a hot-air balloon or hiking in a tropical rain forest somewhere. I wrote a short story called *The Life and Death of the Unicorns*. This may sound harsh, but it was symbolic for me. I love unicorns because they are beautifully magical, but I had gotten to the point that I could not use my imagination like a child anymore. In my story, the unicorns died. It was a tragic illusion of a child's innocence lost. I was in a very dark state of depression at the time. I also had an idea of what if a tiger and panda were bred together, so I drew a picture of it. I called it tiganda. It was a cute idea. I have endless ideas for paintings and writing prompts. I have read many articles and books about creativity and creative thinking. We are all creative in our own ways, not necessarily just the arts. I think it is vital to us as human beings to keep growing and evolving. Writing in a creativity journal can really create new ideas. You would be surprised what ideas you can come up with just by writing in a journal. There are many ways to be inspired creatively. Have tea and coffee with characters for your books, creative geniuses, artists, writers. Go on many adventures.

I gave you a few examples of some of mine. Now it is your turn. For this exercise, I would like you to list some ways *you* like to be creative. It does not have to be art and writing. It can be anything *you* that makes you feel creative. There are countless ways. It can be making music, a science project, cooking a delicious meal, or whatever it is that you like to do. Now think about how the child in you would like to do these things. Write about how you would let the inner child play. Then think about it the next time you do this. Let the magic in!

CHAPTER 2

Imagination Express

Welcome aboard Imagination Express. We are going on an adventure of the mind. Imagine this. What if a tiny airplane with little people flew into your ear and entered your brain? What would they discover? Are you dominantly a left-brained (logical) thinker or more right-brained (artistic and emotional) thinker? Do you think more logically or artistically? I think more dominantly with the right hemisphere of my brain. I am definitely more artistically and emotionally geared. I think of my mind in many different ways. One way is, there is a castle inside my mind with a multitude of doors with different colors and sizes. There is a dragon flying over the castle to protect it. In the tallest tower is a glowing red light, and there is a little girl to keep the castle from crumbling. She keeps my imagination alive. Curious and curiouser. What keeps your imagination alive? Do you see images, words, or numbers? I am not a mathematician, but I see images and words. I guess that is how I am able to make art and write. Creativity turns a caterpillar into a butterfly.

There are many ways to metamorphosize. In my opinion, writing is the first one. I started writing in a journal for therapy in the year of 2000. I have been writing ever since then. I have created ideas for stories and books, original thoughts, quotes, ideas for magazines, stores, poetry, songs, and art. I have written notes for things I have read and watched. My point is that I have written so much after I started journaling twenty-one years ago. Once I started writing, the ideas just come to me like a bee to honey. I never know what adventure my pen will take me on. I may end up in the outback of Australia or a completely new planet no one has ever heard of, not even me. Writing is an art form of a stream or a river with ripples floating gracefully across the winds of time. It is pure bliss when I write something new.

Another way is to take other people's experiences into account. There are thousands of stories to reflect on. I would say, "Follow your heart." Wherever it leads you is your inspiration for good material. The same goes for any creative endeavor, whether it be the arts, cooking, or building a home. As Julia Cameron from *The Artist's Way* says, "Heart is where the art is." You must follow your heart to make art. It does not matter whether it is terrible. It is better to have bad art than no art. Anything creative is art. That does not mean it has to be painting, writing, or music, for example. It can be a science project, researching a subject, or fixing a car. I have lots of paintings because that is what I love. Some of them are pretty good, but some of them are downright horrible. That's how we learn and grow. It just takes time and practice to get better, which goes for anything.

Next, you have to learn to develop ideas for yourself. Reading is a great way to gain knowledge of other people's work. At some point, though, you have to develop your own style and ideas. I have written and written over the years, and I have a lot of materials to refer to now. Writing prompts are a great way to get new material and develop your own ideas. It's important to figure out what is intriguing to you. Are you interested in crime and murder mysteries? Is science more interesting to you? Maybe you love adventure. History is very fascinating. You might prefer laughter over it all. It is just a matter of preference.

It takes passion to create change. For years, I have had mental illness. For the longest time, I thought my life was going to be dull and boring. That was just my perception of it at the time. It has definitely been a journey of the mind. I have to figure out which medications are going to work to decrease symptoms, but they are not a cure-all for everything. I have had to find other things in my life to cope with the illness. Once I started researching books about creativity, I felt hope for a more exciting, fulfilling life. I got more and more passionate about it. I started using my imagination when times get hard. I realized it helped me not be so depressed. I started doing guided meditations on creative visualization, which is where you visualize what you wish to manifest in your life. There are some wonderful guided meditations on YouTube. There are countless books about it. It's a wonderful tool to use. I began to meditate and pray every day. I have experimented with lots of different avenues, such as yoga, kundalini, Zumba, and others to name a few. I became passionate about healing my mental and emotional turmoil. I was able to find various ways to do so. I could focus on something else besides the pain I felt. I read that you can think of your mind as a DVD player. I could fast-forward the parts I didn't like. I also thought of a stop sign, even painted one, and put it beside my bed. When my mind was out of control from mania, I would look at it and think, *Stop thinking*. Then I did some deep breathing to try to calm down. I began to take charge of my negative thoughts. I used many techniques. I imagined myself in a bubble. When negative thoughts came, they would bounce off the bubble. I also saw myself as a ninja who could use karate on the negative thoughts. I still have to work on controlling my mind, but if I don't like something, I try to change the channel. It doesn't always work, but a lot of times, it does. Passion has been a milestone in my recovery.

Curiosity is also another virtue that is important to creativity. Have you ever heard the saying "Curiosity killed the cat"? I think in order to be more creative and imaginative, you have to be curious about the world around you. Find out about all the things that interest you. As I have said, I enjoy painting. It relaxes me and helps me to focus when my mind is spinning out of control, as does writing. I made a list of all the subjects I would like to paint and write about. I was amazed at all the things I came up with. For example, I love the circus, and I thought how cool it would be to be the ringmaster or a trapeze artist. Curiosity is a wonderful thing.

Enthusiasm is also vital to creativity. How can you get anywhere without excitement or enthusiasm about something? I have started many books, but it wasn't until this one that I got really excited about it. I am so enthusiastic to share what I have learned in the hope that it can help those who read it. I think I have had some good ideas, but I follow my heart with this book. My heart leads me what to say. I am not letting my mind override my heart. You have to get excited, something you are passionate about, or it will fizzle out, if not.

I think of our minds like boxes. You put what you want into your box. I mean, you put an image in your memory or a shoebox. Then, when you get ready to do whatever it is you do, you have it there stored away. If I want to paint a panda, I search in my box for a panda bear. If I want to write a story about a rainbow-colored zebra, then I look in my box. I love fantasy, so I have a lot of fairies, elves, dragons, gnomes, kings, queens, princes, and princesses in my box.

Our minds can also be like bank accounts. You can deposit good thoughts, then you can withdraw good thoughts. You can also deposit bad thoughts, and you can withdraw bad thoughts as well.

Then again, our minds are like trees with many branches. Say, you have a thought. Then that thought branches into another thought. Then that thought branches into three more thoughts and so on.

Here are some more ways I came up with to be more artistic.

1. I have found by reading plays and books' dialogues help you pretend you are in the story being told, hence acting.
2. Practice different facial expressions and emotions to become more expressive (not just the basic happy, mad, sad, but a broad scope of emotions).
3. Practice enunciation.
4. Change words around like "scary queen" instead of "dairy queen."
5. Name all the states, continents, and countries.
6. Learn about different cultures.
7. Read books and watch documentaries about subjects that interest you.
8. Read a wide variety of fiction.
9. Paint or do whatever you like to do from the heart.

10. Imagine other lands like Oz from the *Wizard of Oz* or what it would be like to be Edward Scissorhands.
11. Think far into the future or way back into history and imagine what it would be like.
12. Think about colors on a daily basis. Think about the leaves changing color in the fall, the blue sky, lush-green grass, or pretty rocks at a lake or river. Meditate how beautiful God's world is.
13. Look at things from different perspectives.
14. Watch comical movies to forget your problems for a little while. Laughter is the best medicine.
15. Watch dramas to get other perspectives of hardships others have had to endure.
16. Think of a vast amount of characters.
17. Think about what it would be like to be famous.
18. Think about your favorite cartoons.
19. Imagine different weather situations.
20. What kind of charities would you give to, if you could? For example, animal conservation, cancer research, homelessness, foster care, etc.
21. Explore the world.
22. Think about how plants are used for medicine and other things.
23. Think about nostalgic items, such as antiques and collectibles.
24. Think about technology and how our world has changed with it.
25. Think about love and romance.
26. Think about traveling.
27. Think about what inspires you.
28. Think about the fountain of youth and what it would be like if you could go back to your past knowing what you know now.
29. Think about biblical happenings.
30. Think about all the different kinds of food we have.

31. Think about all the different stores and jobs that are available.
32. Think about all the things that we have in this big beautiful universe. Be grateful for what you have.

These are a few of the ideas I use to get my imagination going. I hope this chapter has helped you to get yours going as well. This is a little exercise I chose to help with your imagination. Pick three of the things I listed, or of your own, even better. It does not matter which ones. They might seem wacky, but it can really stimulate your imagination. Pick any form of art you choose. It can be acting, writing, cooking, mechanics, music, or whatever it is that you enjoy. This is your imagination land. Now turn them into some kind of art; your choice. It is whatever you love to do. If it is writing, write a short story. If it is cooking, cook a delicious meal; or if it is music, write a song. Just turn it into some kind of art of your choosing.

CHAPTER 3

How God Helped Me Heal My Trauma with the Gift of Creativity

This chapter has special meaning for me. This is a brief story of how I became mentally ill. My parents separated when I was five. My mom took us to her parents' house in the country, in a small town in Texas. My grandparents were very good to us. My parents had a very volatile back-and-forth relationship, which they divorced two years later. It was very stressful for me since I was the oldest child. My grandfather died the year before they were divorced. This hurt my mom really bad. She lost a husband and her dad. It caused her to be very mentally unstable, which we later found out she had bipolar disorder. She would be depressed, then she wouldn't sleep for days. I had two small sisters by that time. I would try to cheer her up, but I never could. Her grief for the loss of her father and my father was insurmountable. Visitation was a battle. My parents fought over it all the time. However, I have made my amends with my parents. We have better relationships now.

When I was about eight years old is when I began to hear voices. I was sitting in my bedroom one day, and they began talking to me. It scared me so much that I slept with my grandmother that night. But they did not go away. I didn't tell anyone that I heard them because I didn't want to be weird or different from anyone. I kept it secret for years. I tried to be as normal as I could. I loved to sing and dance, so I would parade all over the house singing and dancing, but when I went to my room, where it was quiet, I would hear them. They would tell me their names, and I started acting out their different personalities. I was very different at school. I was extremely quiet and shy. It was like I had two different lives. There was this wildlife of imagination at home, but I was quiet and withdrawn at school. As I got older, the voices became meaner and more aggressive. I wanted them to stop. I began to experiment smoking cigarettes and drinking. Sometimes it helped them go away, but sometimes it made me crazier. I started hanging out with friends every weekend, drinking and smoking pot. That really relieved me from hearing them. One night, a friend gave me cocaine. It was the most wonderful feeling. I didn't hear them anymore, and I had so much energy. It was awesome. Eventually, I was using every day, so I wouldn't hear them tell me how ugly I was, how everyone hated me, and I should kill myself. I felt relief when I drank and did drugs. It was my own personality, and I didn't have to listen to all the horrible things they told me. Still, I told no one I heard them.

I was a straight A student through it all, though. My grandmother had been an English teacher before she had kids. She taught me about English and literature, and she helped me with all my other homework. I did very well. I graduated at seventeen as salutatorian, even with addiction and mental-health issues. She was also an amazing artist! I had the art bug too. I remember watching her paint. It fascinated me, but it wasn't until later that I started painting. I liked doing collages, making crafts, drawing, and reading. I thank God that she was in my life. She was a wonderful, amazing woman. She passed away in 2012. We all miss her so much! God rest her sweet soul.

I met the love of my life when I was seventeen. He was the son of my mom's preacher. He was twenty at the time. We saw each other one day at his dad's church. Our eyes locked, and I hoped we would meet. Later on, we did. It was the summer of 1994, and I had graduated from high school that year. We fell madly in love with each other, and we had the most fun, amazing years together. We had a passionate relationship, like the one similar to *The Notebook*.

The next year, he had to go away. I was put in rehab for the first time at eighteen years old. I needed it so bad. I weighed a mere ninety pounds or less, but I treated it as a joke and was kicked out. The truth was, I was afraid if I quit, the voices would return. I got out, and I did stay sober a few months. I guess the voices were in hibernation. They did not return at that point. My boyfriend asked me to marry him, and I said yes! I was so happy. I loved him so much, and we were in love. We were to be married the next year, but that did not happen. After months of being sober, an old party pal of mine invited me to a party. I consistently told her no, and I was not partying anymore. I told her that I was getting married, and I was very happy. She would not take no for an answer. She repeatedly insisted I needed to go. Finally, I told her that I would go and have a couple of beers, then I would then leave. So we went. I thought I would be there just for a little bit, but that was not the case. They drugged my beer, and I was gang-raped all night until the next day late into the afternoon. When I woke up, I was so sore and beat up that I could hardly put my clothes on. I got a ride home. Then I took a shower, and I scrubbed myself until my skin bled. I lay down on the couch, and I didn't get up, except to use the bathroom for months. I did not eat or anything. My grandmother and mom were so worried. They thought I was going to die. I did finally wake up in April. That happened a couple of days before Halloween. I was not the same person though. I became cold and withdrawn, and I threw myself back into the drug scene, where I experienced many overdoses, black outs, car wrecks, and attempted suicide. I had to go to the mental-health center, because one night, I jumped in front of an eighteen-wheeler. They were able to save me from succeeding. I wanted to die. For many, many years, I was in and out of state hospitals for attempted suicide. One day, I took two bottles of pills. My sister found me on the floor. The ambulance came and got me. They pumped my stomach and sent me to the state hospital. I didn't even realize I had done it. I woke up in the state hospital, and I had to stay there two or three months until they thought I was no longer a danger to myself. They had an art class. I did a wood burning of a horse for my mom. She is passionate about horses. That is where I began to love art again. I wish I could say that it got better when I got out, but it didn't. It got a lot worse. The voices I heard as a child became real. I would end up in weird places and not even know how I got there. It happened all the time. I was on psychiatric medication, but they didn't help. It wasn't until years later that it did.

One year, I went with my aunt to California to get help. I ended up in their psychiatric ward. That is where I met a psychiatrist who suggested that I write in a journal. The first month I was there, all I did was eat and sleep. I felt like I hadn't slept in years. When I did wake up, I began journaling. That was in the year of 2000, and I have done so ever since then. I poured out my toxic thoughts and feelings onto the pages. I wrote about every little thing that happened to me. I only stayed in California for four months. I went home and relapsed for a long time. I kept writing through it all. The more I wrote, the more ideas I had of things to write about. It was my go-to when I couldn't deal with something stressful. Low and behold, it helped. I had been going to therapy and mental-health centers for years, but nothing seemed to help. My writing really started helping me. My art and music also did. I tried to make sense of all the confusion. When I wrote or made art about it, I began to understand my feelings toward things that I had been through. My romantic relationships were never successful at the time. I couldn't understand why I could not make them work. I hated myself for being weird and different. I was later diagnosed with bipolar 1 disorder, borderline personality disorder, and post-traumatic stress disorder. I went to therapy for twenty-five years, and I am still on medication. I will be for the rest of my life. Today, I'm happily engaged. I have finally found real love. Even the most broken hearts can find true love.

In September of 2003, my precious angel was born. I have had a hard time having her, and I nearly died giving birth. I had a vision before I had my blood transfusion, which I was nearly gone. I was in the sky on a cloud. Jesus was on a different cloud. I asked if I was dead, and he told me no. Then I asked why he saved me so many times from near-death experiences. He told me he had a purpose for me to help others, and it hadn't been fulfilled. I was in awe, and I woke up. They handed me my beautiful baby girl. When I looked into her eyes, I knew what my purpose on earth was for, to be the best mom I could be to her. I tried so hard. I played games with her, made art, wrote stories, read to her, watched her on the trampoline, watched her ride her first bike, went to her piano recitals, watched her in gymnastics and sports, gave her birthday parties, went to her school activities, and I did everything I could. Her father and I didn't get along, however. In August of 2011, I tried to commit suicide again. I thought she would be better off without me. The voices were back with a vengeance. I was sent back to the mental hospital. I was not allowed to see her for six months, which was the hardest time of my life, being away from her. I missed her so much. Her father and I broke up, and I decided it was best for her to stay with him so she could have stability. I wasn't stable at all. She lived with him for six years, but I got custody when she was fourteen. I am so very proud of her. She is eighteen now. She is so beautiful inside and out, smart, fun, talented, and she has a very good head on her shoulders. I do not know what I would do without her. She is my reason for living. I love her more than words can say. She is my angel, who saved me. So this is how God helped me heal with the gift of creativity. He gave me a creative mind to help me cope with everything I experienced, and he saved my life so many times that I could count. He gave me my sweet grandmother who nurtured my love for writing and art. He gave me my beautiful daughter at a time when I probably would have died, if I had not gotten pregnant and was able to quit doing everything I was. He gave me a loving family to help and support me. That's really what matters in this life: finding what you love and who you love. There is nothing greater than that!

CHAPTER 4

You are *You*nique

There is nobody like you. This is why I say *you*nique. You are you, and you are unique. That is what this chapter is all about. You may have features that are similar to your family. They are only features. You may have the same eyes as your mother, or you may have the same feet as your grandfather, but no one in the world is exactly like you. Nobody has your DNA. It is specifically you. You have the right to create your life however you wish. No one can take that away from you. There may be situations, such as a bad relationship, that hinders you from feeling free. You could have bad financial issues that keep you from doing what you love. It is all a matter of mind though. If you don't mind, it doesn't matter. My mother used to always tell me that. It wasn't until I got older that I understood it. It is all a state of mind. It is about attitude toward certain things. If you say you can't do it, you won't because you will never try. You have defeated yourself before even trying. I can be quite the negative nelly. I tried to learn guitar for years, but I could never get it. I never practiced, so I shot myself in the foot before I allowed myself to get better. The same goes with a lot of things I have done. I felt like I didn't have proper training to do them, so I just wouldn't even try. However, creativity isn't about copying someone else's work. It is about putting your own stamp on it. I have finally gotten to the point of saying, "So what?" I don't know all the proper techniques, so what? I know I am creative, and that is all that matters. That makes me creative in my own right, and you also. I may not be a superstar, a rocket scientist, or a Victoria's Secret model, but I am me, and I am happy about that. I hope you will see you are creative as well. You are special, no matter what negative things you might have been told. Don't listen to the inner monster or the naysayers that tell you, you will never be anything. Listen to the positive things you hear. You can paint that painting, write that book, draw that portrait, be the head chef of a restaurant, or whatever it is you do. You can sculpt that masterpiece, dance that dance, sing your heart out, or invent that novel idea. The sky is the limit, not even the universe. We live in a ginormous universe.

God created infinity. He is the ultimate creator. Scientists don't even know what are all planets or galaxies that exist. It's enormous. There is a world of knowledge and imagination right in your library or on the internet just waiting for you to tap into. I think being unique is like being in a room of people, but you are the only one wearing sunglasses with purple hair and tattoos. It is unlike anything else. It's like being the only red apple in a group of green Granny Smith apples. It's like being a Lego among porcelain dolls. I am sure you get the point. Being younique is a wonderful, awesome, and amazing thing. You get to be yourself. That is empowering. I had an idea for a song, "Free to be Me." What do you think? How good would it feel to be a more creative version of yourself and not worry about what everyone else's thought about it. Just as American Indians go on a vision quest to discover life's purpose, you are on a quest as well. You can climb that mountain, jump out of the plane, color your hair the color of your choice, or do whatever it is you desire to do. You can go to that motocross event you have always wanted to or listen to a different genre of music you are not familiar with. You can ride that train you have always wanted to go on or take that cruise you have been dying to. You can travel around the world just by going to your library. Books are a fantastic way to use your imagination. There is so much to learn and imagine, just in a book. Now I know money may be a problem to do what it is you are wanting to do. You can read about it and imagine what it would be like.

Then you can start saving money to actually do it. Do not let fear or negative comments get in the way of your dreams. Be fearless. Pray about it. If it is meant to be, God will make a way. The journey could be out of this world. If the inner monster pops its ugly head up, do not listen to the negative comments. It's just the enemy trying to stop you.

My sister gave me a quote a while ago. I love it. It says, "Thoughts are like a garden, you can grow flowers or you can grow weeds." I don't know about you, but I love flowers. They are beautiful and their scent permeates the air. I would much rather grow flowers, but some people like cacti. It's all a matter of preference. My favorite flower is the wildflower, especially the cosmos, which means the universe seen as a well-ordered whole. It reminds me I am just a speck in this humongous universe, which allows me to be humble. It also makes me want to explore the wonders and mysteries of the world. Another quote I like is, "'A reader lives a thousand lives before he dies,' says Jojen. The man who never reads only lives once" (George R. R. Martin, *A Dance with Dragons*).

So what is it you like? Are you a history buff? Are you an athlete? Are you a circus clown? What is it that you like? What makes you *you*nique?

In this exercise, I want you to think of whatever it is and write down twenty things that you like to do and make you *you*nique. They can be realistic or completely unconventional. If it is to ride a hot-air balloon across the world, write it down. If it is to paint a portrait or learn French, write it all down until you have twenty things on your list. You can keep it in a notebook or a folder. Then meditate on these things and think how you can make them a reality or a creative work of art, whichever medium you choose to use.

CHAPTER 5

The Mirror Has Many Faces

What do you see when you look into the mirror? Do you see a good-looking man or woman? Do you feel good about what you see? Do you see a successful person, or do you see a distorted image of yourself?

This chapter is all about the many sides of our personalities. I see many things when I look into the mirror. I see a writer, artist, a mom, a sister, a daughter, a niece, a friend, and the things I should see. However, I also see an adventurer, a visionary, a teacher, an animal lover, a humanitarian, and sometimes a beautiful woman staring back at me. Then there are times I see a monster, a failure, a loser, and all the way around, a horrible person. The mirror can play tricks on our minds, especially with the media always telling us what beautiful or handsome is supposed to look like. We see it on commercials, TV, movies, Facebook, etc. It is everywhere, but it shouldn't make us feel bad about who we are as individuals. Like I said before, we are all unique. There is no one just like us. We each have many sides to us. You may be a lawyer who dreams of surfing. You may be a mom who wants to have her own business. You may dream of being a professional artist or an author of children's books. You may dream of having your own clothing line, being a professional singer, or building your own house. I don't know what your dreams are, but everyone has them.

If you are not pleased with the image you see when you look into the mirror, tell yourself good things about yourself, such as "I have great hair. I love my eyes. I can see a whole world when I look into my eyes. They are mysterious." There are many great things you can tell yourself. Maybe you hate your job, but it pays the bills and gets the things you need. Be proud of yourself for that. It may not be what you dream of, but it is a stepping-stone for better things to come. If you dream of playing the guitar, buy one and try it out. Maybe you have always wanted to be an actor or actress. Are there some classes in your area? Do you love animals. The shelter is full of animals who need love and care. You could adopt a rescue pet. Do you need to lose a little weight to feel better about yourself? There are exercise programs all over YouTube which are a great resource for this if you have access to a computer. Maybe the gym is more your speed.

It is all up to you. I'm not telling you that you need to lose weight. I'm just saying if you don't like the reflection in the mirror, you have the choice to change it. If you are happy what you see, that's awesome; you are winning the self-esteem battle. As humans, we have the potential and ability to change. One person's cup of tea may not suit the other person. That is okay because we are all different. I love ham with syrup on it. You might think it is weird, but I love it. Our differences make us people. It would be a very boring world if we were all the same. Be grateful for all your weird little indiosyncrancies. They make you who you are. I believe in positive affirmations to boost our confidence in ourselves. I started doing them when I was in therapy, and I couldn't stand my reflection in the mirror at the time. I saw a monster inside of me.

I saw a weak, pathetic soul who could not grasp reality. My therapist helped me to see God loved me just as I was. I was sick, and my image was very distorted. I started telling myself good things like "I am beautiful, I am creative, I am God's child, and he loves me." Eventually, I was able to believe those things. When I heard voices to kill myself, I would say good things about myself, and I began to feel better. Now God wants me to try to help you feel better about who you are or what you are having to endure. The enemy wants to kill, steal, and destroy. It says in God's word, but we are saved by the blood Jesus poured out for us.

I imagine myself slaying the ten-headed beast that tries to destroy me. I imagine flying on an eagle, free as the wind. You have to keep telling positive things about yourself. Eventually, the beast will cease to exist. If it comes back, slay him again. Keep slaying it until it leaves you alone. Once you have a fulfilled feeling about yourself, then life can turn around for you. I am not a Bible scholar or anything, but when I pray for the beast to leave me alone, it does.

I'm not saying it is easy. Sometimes, change can be very difficult. I know. I should have died a long time ago, but God isn't finished with me yet. It has been very hard to come to grips with what happened to me, and I hated God for a long time. I even dismissed him in my life. I thought that I didn't need him in my life. You may be thinking the same thing. I'm not trying to force my beliefs on you. I just know that it is God who saved my life so many times. I have heard nothing worth doing is easy, and it isn't. It is possible though. I was hell on wheels trying to walk through my pain for such a long time. I have peace finally. I know it is God who has given it to me. He can give it to you too if you just ask him into your heart. He will come.

There is nothing like the peace of God. Change is inevitable. A friend of mine told me a long time ago, "There are two aspects to life, change or death. The world is changing every day. You can either grasp the changes or die." RIP, Jessie, my friend. He was a wise man. That might sound harsh, but we can die in different ways than just physically, such as shutting down emotionally or in our spirit. I have bipolar disorder. When I have depression, I just want to change things so drastically to feel a different way. You may feel this way too. It is great to change things; just make sure it is positive for you. My Granny Smith used to tell me to tie a big knot and hang on for dear life in times of trouble. She was a very wise woman. We lost her in 2012. It will be nine years in November; bless her sweet soul. We miss her so much! Life can be an awesome experience if you let it.

I've learned it's how you perceive it. I know this book is about being creative, but it is also about believing in yourself. For the longest time, I did not believe in myself. Some things I went through made me cold and bitter. I am waking up on a brighter side of the bed these days; hence the word bed and not in my car, passed out somewhere. I can look in the mirror now, and I like what I see. There is so much variety in this life, which brings me to my next chapter.

First, I would like to ask you to do a couple of exercises. Look in the mirror and tell yourself good things about yourself. Then get out your markers, glitter, paint, glue, or whatever form of media you choose to use. Write down those affirmations you said to yourself, then decorate them however you wish. You can hang your design on the wall, by your mirror, or wherever you wish to remind yourself of all your good features, such as "I am beautiful or handsome, I am creative, I am adventurous, or God loves me." Whatever you need to remind yourself how awesome you are.

CHAPTER 6

Life Is a Rainbow of Flavors

This may sound like a Skittles commercial. You know Skittles taste the rainbow. There are different colors and flavors in a bag of Skittles, and it is similar to what I am talking about—variety. Where would we be without variety? Imagine this, you walk into a Walmart, and everything is black and white. There isn't any color to behold, just black or white. This would be so boring! We are privileged with variety and choices. We don't have to buy the same drinks. There are different types of produce, pastries, meat, sodas, clothing, books, movies, magazines, and this list goes on and on. We have the choice to eat what we want as long as our income allows us too. We don't have to be like the Stepford Wives living in the same houses and doing the same things like robots. We don't always get to choose exactly what or where we want or have our dream car due to finances. We can, however, choose what chips we like or what we want to drink. We can choose what movies and books we like. We have a vast amount of things to choose from. Variety is everywhere we go. We can choose what we like and dislike. We choose what colors we like.

"Life is a rainbow of flavors" is a metaphor I found. I loved it so much. I wanted to include it in this book. There are many aspects to life, just like there are a lot of colors in the world. It is all around us. On a sunny day, the sky is so blue. In the spring, the trees and grass are many shades of green. There are numerous shades of colors: royal blue, sky blue, turquoise, forest green, yellow green, red violet, orange, pumpkin orange, and the list continues. There are fluorescent colors, metallic, silver swirls, multicultural, glow in the dark, and there is even a color in the Crayola crayon box called macaroni and cheese. Can you imagine? They have given names, such as asparagus green to outer-space blue. I love it.

A donut shop has many flavors of pastries. They have chocolate donuts, jelly-filled donuts, donuts with sprinkles, éclairs, and many more. Life has many flavors as well.

You can choose what pizza you prefer. There is such an assortment of choices and what you desire for toppings on pizza.

There is a menagerie of restaurants to select from. There are tons of stores to shop at. There are thousands of hobbies to pick from. Inspiration can be anywhere.

Look how many different people there are in the world. I have met a lot of interesting people in my life. Some people would have thought they were strange, but I understood where they were coming from. At first, I thought they were strange, but they were just unique. Normalcy is different for everyone. I didn't grow up in the city. I grew up on the outskirts of a small town in Texas, but I was never a normal "country girl." Once I went to the city, I was amazed and astonished but, in a way, felt at home. There were so many rad people to meet and so much cool stuff to do. There are so many types of people. There are the intellectuals, the entertainers, athletes, and the artistic type, which I meshed well with. There are the introverts and the extroverts. Some people are short, while others are tall. There are a variety of cultures and languages. There is a vast world of spiritual practices, which I respect, although I believe in God the creator. There are dreamers and realists. It would take forever to talk about all the differences of people, with all our indiosychrancies and imperfections that make us who we are. That is a beautiful thing. I am talking about a world of people, such as scientists, artists, historians, lawyers, bankers, doctors, etc. We need to come to a point in this life where we respect other's differences. We all have our own personalities and personas. Wouldn't it be great if we could accept, or at least, respect each other's differences?

Dogs and cats each have their own personalities also. No two are alike. Some are skittish, while others are friendly. Some will bite, but others are as sweet as they can be. I say dogs and cats, but I actually mean all animals. Each have their own unique personalities; giraffes have super long necks. Penguins look like they are wearing little tuxedos. Turtles have hard shells to protect them from predators. Chameleons blend in with their surroundings by changing colors. Lions and tigers are majestic, while hyenas are scavengers. Variety comes in all sizes, shapes, and colors. God created it this way.

There are limitless things you can do to be more creative. There are a number of hobbies to practice. There are inspiring subjects everywhere. Here is a list of some of the hobbies out there:

1. New languages
2. Remote-control helicopters
3. Puppets
4. Juggling
5. Magic tricks
6. Model trains, cars, and airplanes
7. Build with Legos
8. Bikes
9. Volleyball
10. Fishing
11. Walking
12. Hiking
13. Mountain climbing
14. Dancing
15. Swimming
16. Soccer
17. Astronomy
18. Model rockets
19. Aquariums
20. Museums
21. Family tree
22. Woodworking
23. Freelance writing
24. Crafts to make and sell
25. Cake decorating

26. Carpentry
27. Collecting items
28. Jewelry making
29. Baking
30. Pottery
31. Candle making
32. Soap making
33. Digital art
34. Cooking
35. Doll making
36. Scrapbooking
37. Sewing
38. Gardening
39. Dollhouses
40. Critiquing movies
41. Board games
42. Bingo
43. Book club
44. Acting
45. Frisbee golf
46. Writing children's books
47. Camping
48. Gazing at the stars
49. Sports
50. Video games

These are just a few of the multitudes of hobbies to try. It would take a lifetime to list all of them. I am wrapping up this chapter, but I hope I helped you see how life is a rainbow of flavors.

For this exercise, I want you to get stack of magazines and look through them. Then cut out twenty images that appeal to you. Take note of why you like them. Then on poster board, glue them on as a collage. This will be your dream board. You can refer to it anytime you are feeling stuck. It will remind you of all the splendid variety we have in this world.

CHAPTER 7

Give Your Dreams Wings

I don't know about you, but I love creatures with wings. I love birds, butterflies, fairies, and dragons, to name a few. They just seem so free soaring through the air, like an eagle flying effortlessly through the sky. Our dreams can fly also if we let them. I know fairies and dragons are fictional, but I like fantasy. Wishes can fly, but only if you give them wings. When was the last time you truly believed in something so much, it grew wings and took flight? My dream for this book is that it will help you believe in your dreams again. If one didn't work out, then maybe it is time to try a new one. Don't let failure stand in your way. If you fall, get up and try again. You deserve good things for your life. I don't know what your dream may be, but if you believe in it enough, it could come true. To be an artist is to live, feel, then to express. It is seeing ordinary things in life you rarely see. If a person becomes mentally inactive, it can be exhausting. When I am in a depression phase, I get so tired to do anything, even getting out of bed. It makes me physically ill also. Artists and creatives usually live a long time. My grandmother was an amazing artist. She lived to be ninety-five. Everything you do creates a sense of accomplishment, which, of course, makes anyone feel better about what they are doing and who they are. It allows you to feel a sense of empowerment and freedom. Your dreams could be like buried treasure. You must go an adventure and find it. It is not gone forever, just buried. Imagine you have to find it before the pirates steal it. You have the map and the key; you just need to rediscover it. Let the winged creature of your dream take you on a journey through the clouds.

Look at every day as a blank canvas. You have to fill it with color. I struggle with that a lot. I want each day to be a new adventure, but I have to create it. Sometimes, my creativity is stifled. I get really depressed when this happens, but I just keep pushing on. I think everybody should reach to the stars, hold them in your hands, and let them shine. Here is an inspirational poem I wrote:

Happiness Today

> I know I can do it
> There's nothing to it
> Dreaming my worries away
> Just think of all the things there is to love
> Life is much better today
> So dream a little dream
> Wish a little wish
> Add a drop of passion to your dish
> Watch the sorrow melt away
> Voila, you have happiness today.

I like to go to this poem when I am feeling blue. I hope it will help you too.

You are the pilot of your airplane. Let it take you where you want to go. Destiny is right around the corner. What is destiny, you may ask? Is it something you catch in the air? Is it something to put on to wear? Where do you find it? How do you find yours? I believe it has already been determined by our creator. It is written in the stars for you. It is up to us to seek it out. It is what we go through in life, what we become, shaping who we are, where we have been, and what we have seen. It is finding beauty and truth. Truth is beauty. It is being true to ourselves and to others. Beauty isn't only skin-deep. Sometimes we have to swim in deeper waters to find true beauty. Yes, it is good to look good, but vanity is not. The exterior of our bodies will fade. I believe true beauty is giving back to others. Otherwise, you could be searching all your life for something that is not going to bring you happiness. For a while, it might bring instant gratification, just like drugs and alcohol. It will not last long, though. Then you have to keep getting another fix for that feeling. Before you know it, you have to have it to feel normal. It's a vicious cycle, and it is very hard to stop. I pray for anyone who may be going through that vicious cycle right now. It is very hard to quit, but it is possible. You may need professional help, but there is hope. Dreams give us wings. Dreams can set us free. It is looking toward the future and making the best of life we can with what we have. It is wanting a better life for our children. It is wanting a better life for our loved ones. It is reaching for the stars. It is flying above the clouds. Dreaming can give you an incredible feeling in your spirit. It allows us to see the impossible really is possible if you don't stop believing. Let your dreams take flight. Imagine all the wondrous things you can. Think big.

For this exercise, I would like you to draw a picture of your dream, then attach wings to it. It doesn't have to be good. It can be a stick figure, if you want, but this will remind you of your dream taking flight. If your dream is to be a singer, draw a person with a microphone. Then draw wings on it. It may sound silly, but this is your dream. Give it wings.

CHAPTER 8

Never Give Up

Sometimes life has a way of taking our dreams away from us, but we can't let this stop us from pursuing them. My grandmother always told me, "Can't never could." Maybe you have been knocked down a few times or even ten thousand times, then brush off the dust and try again. My mom's philosophy is "It's like riding a horse. If you get thrown off, you have to get back on, or you might not ever."

It is like remarrying someone after you have had the first divorce. If you don't try again, then you take the risk of being lonely the rest of your life. You have to keep trying. Don't ever give up. Say, you are a cake decorator, and your cakes just look like a big blob. It's okay; just keep practicing, and eventually, you will either get better or not. If you don't, then try something else. That is what's wonderful about dreams. We can change them. If you don't like something, change it. Don't ever give up. Keep going. Keep moving ahead. Don't let the woes of life defeat you.

When I was eighteen, I wanted to be a model and move to New York. I went to modelling school and graduated. My class and I did a runway show at the Radisson Hotel in Dallas. I really thought I was going to be able to go to New York to be a high-fashion model, but circumstances happened that were out of my control, and I never made it there. I was too sick to go. I have a new life and new dreams now. I realized it was not meant for me to be a model. I didn't give up on my dreams, but they changed. Life is always evolving, whether we want it to or not; it does. Sometimes I feel like giving up, but I keep pressing on. You should too. There will always be setbacks, but just keep moving forward.

I know a sweet, special little girl named Olivia, who has Rett syndrome. She was diagnosed when she was two and a half. She deteriorated quickly within a month her mom told me, but when I saw her pictures, she was a happy child. She has a wonderful, loving mother who never gave up on her. It must be her love and support who helped her to keep going, even though, I couldn't imagine how hard it was for either of them. They never gave up. She was a true inspiration to so many people.

I also know someone who has had muscular dystrophy since he was five. The doctors said he would not live to be twenty-one, but he is well into his thirties now. He is a cool guy. He loves sports and has met many of the players personally. His mom and dad are wonderful people. They have taken him to a lot of games. His spirit is bigger than the universe. He is an inspiration to never give up. Keep fighting for another day.

I love the song "The Eye of the Tiger" by Survivor. It was the *Rocky* theme song. You have to fight for what you want. You go through your trials. Everyone does. If a tiger gave up, he would starve. He relentlessly pursues his prey. It is sad, but it is nature. The ones who don't give up are the survivors. Live with the eye of the tiger. Pursue your dreams, if that is what you want. Sometimes there is no easy way out. I never in a million years thought I would have to fight for my life, but I did. I was able to come out stronger than I have ever been. I think of the people out there with terminal illnesses. I can't imagine how that must be, but when they give up, it could be the end. If that is you, don't give up. Keep praying for another day.

If people had given up, we wouldn't have the technology we have today. We wouldn't have cell phones, computers, or even electricity for that matter. If Benjamin Franklin had given up, we would not have electricity. Can you imagine life without electricity? I wouldn't want to. We would be stuck in the pioneer days. Albert Einstein would not have discovered the theory of relativity. We would live in a much different world if they had given up. We can't give up. Fight the fight with all your might. Fight fire with fire. You deserve to fight for your dreams. Believe in yourself. Have faith. Never give up. Don't let the negativity bring you down. We change as life changes. It is time to be bold for what you want out of it.

In this exercise, I want you to make a bucket list. This is a list of all the things you want to do before you die. It can be as long or short as you want. Try to list everything you can think of.

CHAPTER 9

Enjoy the Journey

Life is a journey. You have to find out what makes it a happy one. We have discussed some of the ways to look at it differently. Always look at life with your eyes wide open. Use all your senses, enjoy every morsel of food you eat, see that beautiful sunset, hear that wonderful music, touch your partner sensually, smell that delicious meal cooking, and listen to the patters of your heart. Never let anyone squash your dreams or tell you something you did is garbage. Remember, you are *you*nique.

There is much variety in this life. Be grateful for breath to live another day and make the most of every day. Reach for the stars. You are an awesome creative soul. Find out what your passion is and go for it. Don't let failure detour you from your dreams. Don't let anyone make you feel less than you are. Life is about making mistakes and trying to learn from it. Don't beat yourself up for not being perfect. Only God is perfect; we are human beings. I have made tons of mistakes, but I am not going to let it destroy the rest of my life. I have dusted myself off, and I am back in the game. I have anted up to another hand of cards. It is a new chapter in my life, and I'm enjoying it.

The scene in the movie has changed. If I were to write a screenplay for a movie, it would be a lifetime movie. I have overcome many obstacles. I am still here. If I can do it, so can you. I want to enjoy the journey for the rest of my life. I know I will make more mistakes.

That is just a part of life. The sailing will be smoother this time. The water won't be quite as choppy without the wind blowing me in a hundred different directions. I'm not where I want to be, but I thank God I'm not where I used to be. I am so grateful for my beautiful daughter. I thought I would never get custody back to her, but I did. I did not give up. I got better, and I did get her back. I'm thankful for my family who loves and supports me, even though I know I'm very difficult to love or get along with sometimes. If you do not have any family, I care about you. That is why I wrote this book, to try to help others live a life they love. I thank God for giving me a creative mind. It has helped me cope with things that were out of my control. It gave me a new perspective of how to view life with severe mental illness and how to rise above it. I still struggle. Mental illness isn't easy to live with on a daily basis. Sometimes I just want it to end, but my daughter needs me. I keep fighting every day for her. I'm so grateful I was blessed with such a wonderful grandmother who loved me, my sisters, our family, and so many others. She was a true jewel. She was a lady with endless amounts of love. I miss her every day, but I know she is at peace and is not in pain anymore. Think of all the things you do well and all the things you have yet to do. Think about what makes you smile and feel happy. Imagine you are climbing a mountain, and you are halfway there. You just have to keep climbing to reach the top. It is possible. It is doable. I'm climbing my mountain every day. Eventually, I will reach the top. You will as well. You have to keep pushing on. Some things that make me smile are my daughter's eyes lighting up when she does something she is proud of herself. It puts joy in my heart to see her happy. When I get calls and texts from my family, that makes me happy. Some other things are Chinese food, a beautiful sunset, the moon and stars, my art and writing, music, and just feeling truly alive.

I love my family, but I don't get to see my immediate family very often. When we do get to see each other, it is such a joyous time. What is a happy time for you? If you have dropped out of the race, maybe it is time to get back in and try again. Let inspiration grab a hold of you and shake a little bit. Don't quit the game. It is not over. Enjoy the ride. Let your hair fly with the wind blowing it. See all the little treasures God has gifted us with. Breathe that breath of fresh air. Look at the sky and let your mind wander about all the mysteries of the world. Are we really alone, or do other beings exist? Think about the natural wonders of the world. There are many things to ponder. Dreams aren't over when obstacles arise. Obstacles can make dreams bloom like a beautiful flower in the sun. Sometimes you just have to look in the cookie jar. Be yourself, no matter what it is. It is much better than being fake and being something you are not.

It has taken me a long time to be who I really am. Through the years, I have been many people. I couldn't accept who I was. I tried to be something I wasn't, but it never worked out. I was the party girl for many years. It almost killed me because I couldn't' grasp reality. I am an artist and a writer. That is who I am meant to be. You will find out who your authentic self is. You will feel like a weight has been lifted when you do. Enjoy the journey.

For this exercise, write down a list of ten things that make you happy. Then write a letter to your past and future self. You can explain to your past self what you wish you had done differently. You can tell your future self what things you want to manifest and where you hope to be by then. Then put on some music and dance and sing your heart out, celebrating who you are. Maybe try a different genre of music that you never listen to. Enjoy your journey of living for today.

CHAPTER 10

God Is Real

I was raised in a Christian household, but it was far from perfect. Our life was very dysfunctional. We did not know it, but our mom was mentally ill. She had bipolar disorder, also known as manic depression. Her moods were very unstable. She would be so depressed she would cry and sleep all day, or she would be so manic that she didn't sleep for days. I had it too, but I didn't know until I was older. I also have borderline personality disorder and post-traumatic stress disorder. My mom was a Christian, but her illness caused her to do things to harm us. I know it was not intentional. She loved us, but her illness was in control. My grandmother always went to church every Sunday. She was a very religious woman. My illnesses caused me to rebel and deny God. I suffered the consequences of my actions. However, I have given my life back to God. I know it was only by his grace and mercy that I am alive today. I don't know many scriptures. I wish I did, but my favorite is Jeremiah 29:11, "'For I know the plans I have for you,' declares the Lord, 'plans to prosper you and not harm you, plans to give you hope and a future.' Then shall ye call upon me, and ye shall go and pray unto me, and I will hearken unto you."

It has taken me a long time to repent of my sins and repent toward God, but I finally have. This may not be for you. If it isn't, I respect that. You may believe in the universe, a goddess, or you may be Buddhist or something else. That is fine. I'm not asking you to believe the way I do. I mean, it would be great if you did. God loves all of us equally, but he does give us free will. After all the near-death experiences I have had, I know Jesus is my saviour. God made me creative so I can share creative healing with you. He also made me understanding, and I do not expect for you to change your spiritual practices unless you want to. I have been through all I have to help others using creativity as my gift. I know that today. Some nights, when I am all alone, God comforts me in his arms while I cry myself to sleep.

He loves you too, but he will not force you to follow him. I used to be very rebellious. I was a hellion, but I have paid the consequences and then some for not listening to wisdom. I am not going to get too preachy. I always hated that. I don't try to push my beliefs on anyone. If he is calling to you, I would listen, but no one is going to force you.

My spiritual awakening happened this summer. It was the most wonderful and beautiful thing I have ever experienced. I finally feel peace. For years, people have tried to push their beliefs on me, and I retaliated that much more, but when I met God for myself, my perspective has changed forever. At last, I am free. I do not judge what people believe. It is your life, and you may believe what you want to believe. This is how I have chosen to believe for now on. It has taken a lot of anguish and misery to get here, but I know God is real, now. Nature is a wonderful example of how to live our lives. I am like water. Water can carve rocks, turn iron into rust, and create a new path when it has nowhere to go. I was inspired when I watched *Memoir of a Geisha*, and she talked about being like water. That is how I am, like water. What element do you think you are?

This is a small chapter. I do not like to force my beliefs on anyone, but I know God has a purpose for all our lives. Jesus died so we could be forgiven of our sins.

For this exercise, I want you to meditate, pray, or however you give thanks for all the blessings you have in your life. Then write down all the things you are grateful for. You can look back on this when you are having a hard time, to remind you how blessed you are.

CONCLUSION

In summary, there are more things that have saved my life. God, the people I love, art, writing, and music. Art and writing have changed the way I perceive the world around me. If I still thought the way I did, I would be in a black hole, sucking the life out of me with every dark thing there is, like monsters, vampires, and worms eating my brain. I have learned to think differently about myself and this magnificent universe. I hope I have helped you too. It has been a journey. I love adventures. Remember, you are *you*nique. No one can take that away from you. We all have different personalities. There is a world of variety out there just waiting for you to discover.

I would not be writing this if I had given up. I would probably be in some dark hole, six feet under, if I had given up. I didn't. I chose to fight. Never give up on your dreams. Let them have wings and fly you to your destiny. Let your imagination take you to interesting places.

Enjoy your journey in this thing we call life. Make movies of it. The only person who can really stop you is you. We only get one life on Earth. This is the only chance we get to be here. Make it a fun, interesting, memorable one. Try to live every day as if it is your last. We never know when our time will be over. Make the most of it. Find your star—Ringo Starr from The Beatles. Find your passion and go for it. If you fail a hundred times, get back up a hundred and one. Never ever give up! You never know what's around the next corner.

ABOUT THE AUTHOR

Tina Melton is a self-taught writer and artist who lives with her fiance and beautiful daughter in Texas. She has always had a passion for writing, art, and music. She loves fantasy, nature, and going to the lake. She enjoys painting and writing in a journal, which she has done since 2000. She loves writing short stories, poems, and songs. She has found creative outlets are therapeutic, yet fun, as well. She believes everyone is creative. Her motto is life is a gift, and we shouldn't waste it.

Printed in the USA
CPSIA information can be obtained
at www.ICGtesting.com
LVHW030213280124
769952LV00002B/175